D1266447

37 211102

GT
871
M38
1997

La Mode Illustrée
FASHION PLATES
in Full Color

Edited by
Florence Leniston

*Introduction and translations
of original descriptions by*
JoAnne Olian

DISCARDED

DOVER PUBLICATIONS, INC.
Mineola, New York

JUN 23 1998

NORMANDALE COMMUNITY COLLEGE
LIBRARY
9700 FRANCE AVENUE SOUTH
BLOOMINGTON MN 55431-4399

Copyright

Copyright © 1997 by Dover Publications, Inc.
All rights reserved under Pan American and International Copyright Conventions.

Published in Canada by General Publishing Company, Ltd., 30 Lesmill Road, Don Mills, Toronto, Canada.
Published in the United Kingdom by Constable and Company, Ltd., 3 The Lanchesters, 162–164 Fulham Palace Road, London W6 9ER.

Bibliographical Note

La Mode Illustrée Fashion Plates in Full Color, first published by Dover Publications, Inc., in 1997, reproduces the color plates originally published in *La Mode Illustrée,* 1886. A new Introduction and paraphrases of the original descriptions have been specially prepared for this edition.

Library of Congress Cataloging-in-Publication Data

La mode illustrée fashion plates in full color / edited by Florence Leniston; introduction and translations of original descriptions by JoAnne Olian.
     p.   cm.
  Originally published in La mode illustrée. 1886.
  ISBN 0-486-29819-1 (pbk.)
  1. Fashion—France—History—19th century—Pictorial works.
I. Leniston, Florence. II. Mode illustrée.
GT871.M58   1997
391'.00944'09034—dc21   97-22623
                                               CIP

Manufactured in the United States of America
Dover Publications, Inc., 31 East 2nd Street, Mineola, N. Y. 11501

INTRODUCTION

The most striking novelty in the eighth and last Impressionist exhibition in 1886 was the large landscape with figures, "Sunday Afternoon on the Island of La Grande Jatte," by Georges Seurat. The quintessence of the current mode, Seurat's fashionably attired women, as blissfully unaware of their enormously protruding bustles as store mannequins, glide serenely across the canvas. This curious silhouette, so far removed from the modern esthetic and so antithetical to the human anatomy, was to remain in vogue from 1883 to 1888, attaining its most exaggerated form in 1885.

La Mode Illustrée Fashion Plates in Full Color affords a unique opportunity to observe a complete year of fashion, with the range of colors and fabrics suitable to each season. The weekly color plates from the deluxe edition of *La Mode Illustrée* for 1886 provide an in-depth view of mid-eighties fashion for today's reader, who cannot help but think of the freedom these toilettes must have given the dressmaker, despite the confines of the current silhouette, to create endless variations on a theme. The complexity of construction required that dresses have at least two skirts, over which a tunic or a drapery, often in the form of a polonaise, was draped over the hips, ending in a pouf over the bustle in the rear. Skirts had no trains and were the same length all around, barely skimming the ground. The corsage, or bodice, was usually open to reveal a chemisette and often a plastron as well.

The fashion was described brilliantly by Proust in *Remembrance of Things Past* in Swann's first impression of Odette de Crecy: "... as for her figure, and she was admirably built, it was impossible to make out its continuity (on account of the fashion then prevailing, and in spite of her being one of the best-dressed women in Paris) for the corsage, jetting forwards in an arch, as though over an imaginary stomach, and ending in a sharp point, beneath which bulged out the balloon of her double skirts, gave a woman, that year, the appearance of being composed of different sections badly fitted together; to such an extent did the frills, flounces, the inner bodice follow, in complete independence, controlled only by the fancy of their designer or the rigidity of their material, the line which led them to the knots of ribbons, falls of lace, fringes of vertically hanging jet, or carried them along the bust, but nowhere attached themselves to the living creature who, according as the architecture of their fripperies drew them towards or away from her own, found herself either strait-laced to suffocation or else completely buried."

The bustle, fashionable in the 1870s, disappeared completely in 1880, to be replaced by the wasp-waisted, form-fitting, hobble-skirted princesse dress, before enjoying a five-year revival beginning in 1883. The new bustle was much more extreme than its predecessor, a gently curving form ending in a graceful train. In 1887, *La Mode Illustrée* commented on some of these eccentric excrescences: "The tournure is not near the point of disappearing. Some completely comical ones are even seen: those which affect the form of the horn which a rhinoceros wears on his forehead; others representing two spread wings placed at the small of the back." This bustle, so high and angular that one could balance a tea set on it, and indeed women's clothing in general, was much more hard-edged than it had been a decade earlier.

Besides the bustle, hallmarks of mid-eighties fashion were tailoring, pleats, severe military collars, jacket-bodices with revers and plastrons, and asymmetrical closings and drapery on both corsage and skirt. While some of these components were borrowed from male attire, the pointed cuirasse bodice accentuating a rigidly corseted waist, further emphasized by the amplitude of drapery around the hips, was pure femininity.

Textiles, an integral part of the fashion, were nearly upholstery weight and included satins; plain, cut, and patterned velvets; ribbed wools; sicilienne, "one of the family of ribbed silks known as faille, bengaline, grosgrain and ottoman;" jacquard-patterned and striped or brocaded silks. Plush was a favorite, "... entirely tasteful for daytime and also combines well with net for ball toilettes."

An elegant costume was composed of a minimum of two materials and often three. Embellishments of lace, ball-fringe, braid, embroidery, tassels, beading, ribbons, or combinations of these were de rigueur. *La Mode Illustrée* remarked that there was not a single fabric which could not be utilized in the modern toilette, while hitherto unimagined combinations were also to be in style, even going so far as to suggest taking apart two or three outmoded costumes and combining them into one new ensemble.

The plastron, actually a vest or a simulated vest or vestee, was such an important characteristic of 1886 fashion that *La Mode Illustrée* devoted the better part of a January column to its many variations: "The aim of the present mode seems to be the pursuit of perpetual change: to vary unceasingly the appearance of the toilette is the medium employed to attain this goal which can be achieved in part with plastrons of every genre which are worn with every corsage. The nature of these plastrons varies according to their purpose, since they are worn with simple day dresses as well as with dressy evening wear, with high-necked corsages as well as with corsages open in front, where they fill the void. Plastrons for the morning are made of soft silk, velvet, medium or dark-colored plush; for the evening ... how to interpret or to describe them? They are made of net, gauze, crepe, white, black or colored lace, white or pale colors with silk embroidery, above all with beads, also pearls (imitation), of tiny coral or garnet beads."

The range of color was consistent with the weight of the materials, favoring deep tones such as browns, garnet, ivy, bronze, and navy, sometimes paired with clashing contrasting shades. The general effect was of somber opulence, or richness, reflecting the eighties predilection for eclectic interiors crammed with a mix of dark, heavily tufted and fringed upholstery, massive carved furniture, and exotica from the Middle East.

Eclecticism ran rampant through the pages of *La Mode Illustrée* in 1886. Historic and exotic references abounded. Sleeves were slashed, puffed and, sometimes left hanging, attached only at the shoulder, in medieval fashion. Lacing on corselets and corsages was popular. Equally fashionable were Louis XIII, Louis XV, pompadour floral patterns, Louis XVI fichus, Persian prints, and Greek pleats (pleats on the bodice which taper from bust to waist).

It is somewhat of a paradox that when a ten-story skyscraper had already been erected in Chicago, the first gas vehicle had been manufactured by Daimler-Benz, and the Orient Express was carrying passengers from Paris to Istanbul, that the past, rather than the exigencies of the modern world, should have been the source of inspiration for the *dernier cri* in fashion. However, periodicals such as *La Mode Illustrée* were fueled by innovations and the passionate desire to be *à la mode*. Since a new fashion is copied rapidly, its very popularity soon renders it demodè, so that the fashionable woman is constantly obliged to be on the lookout for the next one, which, should it prove to be merely a variation of the dress of an earlier epoch, has nonetheless acquired an aura of freshness and novelty in its new guise. Oscar Wilde's witty epigram offers a succinct explanation for the eternal quest: "After all, what is fashion? It is usually a form of ugliness so intolerable that we have to alter it every six months."

JoAnne Olian
New York City

NOTES ON PLATES

These notes have been paraphrased from the original French descriptions. French terms and special fashion terms are defined in the glossary on pages xii–xiii.

No. 1. Toilettes de Mme. Coussinet, rue Richer, 13. (January 3)

LEFT: Dress of plain ivy-colored sicilienne and sicilienne with chamois-colored dots. The underskirt is of figured sicilienne. The overdress, of plain sicilienne, is draped in front, caught up at the hip, and draped in back. A pleated panel of the same plain sicilienne falls vertically on one side. The round corsage, with an ivy-colored velvet belt, crosses and is open over a figured plastron. Drapery, collar, and cuffs of ivy-colored velvet. RIGHT: Visiting toilette of striped velvet and faille française in a deep shade of heliotrope. The underskirt, of faille française, is trimmed with two panels of striped velvet that cross in front and are flanked by two wide, flat pleats. A faille drapery trims the front of the skirt. The round corsage is adorned with a wide striped velvet sash, tied at the side and ending in fringe. The corsage with double revers opens over a striped velvet plastron.

No. 2. Coiffures de Mr. Camille, 9, rue du 4 Septembre. (January 10)

TOP, LEFT AND RIGHT: The hair is arranged in front in a cluster of ringlets and a frisette on the forehead. In back, the hair is divided into intertwined locks and held in place with jewel-headed pins. A spray of plumes, held by ribbon rosettes, is placed atop the head. CENTER: Fancy-dress headdress. Powdered hair. Garde-française chapeau of red plush, embroidered in gold, topped with a bouquet of red roses and plumes. BOTTOM LEFT: Fancy-dress coiffure. Louis XV. Powdered hair with a pouf of pale pink ribbon and a white aigrette. BOTTOM RIGHT: Greek headdress, executed in red and olive striped silk, bordered with a fringe of sequins. The hair is curled under this headdress.

No. 3. Toilettes de Mme. Coussinet, rue Richer, 43. (January 17)

LEFT: Visiting toilette of kingfisher blue jaspé plush. Satin underskirt of a lighter shade of the same color, with an inset embroidered in chenille and beads on one side. The plush overdress is open over this inset; it falls straight on this side and is extremely draped on the opposite side. The simple corsage is closed on the bias and seems to be laced with a moiré ribbon that continues onto the skirt, appearing to lace the two sides of the skirt. RIGHT: Visiting dress of fancy velvet in a shade of campeche wood. The main skirt is composed of three panels of striped velvet, cut on the bias in such a fashion as to create wide diagonal stripes. These panels are edged with ball fringe of multicolored beads. A long habit of plain velvet descends to the hem in back, forming a sort of skirt arranged in wide pleats. The corsage of this habit, very short in front, is cut out in two points at the center of the bust, allowing a glimpse of a striped gilet. The striped pouf passes between the two tails of the habit. Plain velvet hat matching the habit is trimmed with plumes in several shades of the same color.

No. 4. Toilettes de Mme. Delaunay, rue Godot de Mauroy, 49. (January 24)

LEFT: Evening gown. Lower skirt of pale pink faille adorned with a deep shirred flounce of pink gauze. The upper part of the skirt front is covered with a tablier of white lace. Corsage and train of red velvet. The front of the pointed décolleté corsage is decorated with white lace falling to the point of the corsage. Velvet epaulets with lace drapery serve as short sleeves. The tablier is trimmed on both sides and at the hem with bouquets of roses ending in pale pink ribbons. RIGHT: Short dress of sapphire-colored moiré striped with figured cashmere and matching plain moiré. Plain moiré tunic with wide rosettes of striped goods, arranged in back to simulate a pouf. Plain moiré corsage trimmed with bands of striped moiré. The corsage opens over a figured plastron. Revers, sleeves, and small collar made of bands taken from the moiré stripes.

No. 5. Travestissements de Mme. Pelletier-Vidal, rue Duphot, 17. (January 31)

FANCY DRESS COSTUMES. LEFT: Flower-seller (10- to 12-years of age). Short dress of "pigeon's throat" (purple) changeable taffeta. Pleated tablier of Corinth grape satin. Round corsage of black velvet with heart-shaped neckline, half-long sleeves edged with a lace ruche. On the corsage, a white muslin fichu trimmed with lace. Black velvet ribbon at the neck. On the head, a high muslin coif, encircled by a wide black velvet ribbon. On the arm, a large, flat basket filled with flowers. Blue stockings. Shoes of black leather with buckles. CENTER: Indian snake charmer (young woman). Short dress of white voile, pleated all around. Tight-fitting princesse dress of light cerise plush, satin, or velvet, with low square corsage and skirt caught up all around, longer on one side than the other. A long Indian shawl in pale shades is draped around the hips. Short sleeves of mousseline edged with gold braid. The same braid is around the neckline of the corsage. On the shawl and corsage, a large undulating snake. Snake bracelets. Necklace of gilded sequins. Little toque of the same goods and color as the dress; the hair curled and flowing. In the hand, a feather fan. RIGHT: Louis XIII costume (little boy, 7- to 9-years of age). Wide pantaloons and justaucorps of pale blue velvet. Wide fawn-color leather belt. Soft, high boots of the same leather. White lace ruffled collar and cuffs. Wide-brimmed felt hat trimmed with large white plumes. In the hand, a tall cane and deerskin gauntlets.

No. 6. Toilettes de Mme. Coussinet, rue Richer, 43. (February 7)

LEFT: Visiting toilette of chartreuse-colored faille française and plush. The skirt, arranged all around in vertical pleats, is made of plush. The tunic, of the faille, is arranged in stepped pleats; caught up on one side, it falls straight on the other. It is outlined with narrow braid and beaded ball fringe in the same color as the faille. The pointed corsage, of plush, is trimmed with faille revers edged with ball fringe, opening on a guimpe of pleated smooth white crepe. Around the neck, a man's cravat of the same crepe. RIGHT: Dinner toilette for young girl. Dress of sky blue victoria. The skirt, in wide pleats, is caught up at one side; this gap is filled in by a drapery of victoria enclosed between revers of white voile embroidered with forget-me-nots. High-necked corsage in the same voile, with little flat basques. On the bodice, two wide bretelles of victoria are fastened at the shoulder and attached to a corselet of the same stuff.

No. 7. (February 14)

LEFT: Dress of plush and faille in two shades of copper. The skirt is composed of alternating flat panels of plush and faille. The plush panel on the left side is caught up on a satin panel and held by three ribbon bows. Little black silk gauze mantelet, pleated vertically with sleeves of black faille striped with black plush. The lower edge of the mantelet is trimmed with a wide piece of Chantilly, surmounted by a braid of jet ball fringe. Each tail ends with a tassel or ball fringe of jet. Bonnet of copper-colored plush with an aigrette of feathers shaded from copper to sulphur. RIGHT: Promenade toilette. Skirt of sapphire velvet with fine red stripes and red edging at the hem. Tunic of sapphire vigogne, caught up and held on the left side. This tunic, with flat pleats, is trimmed with sapphire-colored passementerie ornaments. High-necked corsage with long sleeves, with three points in front, made of the same goods as the skirt. Red velvet collar. Hat of sapphire plush faced and trimmed with red velvet.

No. 8. (February 21)

LEFT: Dinner toilette of "alicante-color" (red) bengaline and moiré. The plain petticoat is of moiré. Polonaise of bengaline gathered on one side only, held at the waist by a belt, falling straight in flat pleats held by a very large passementerie ornament of multicolor beads. The fronts of the polonaise are pleated on the shoulders and open in a heart shape over a plastron of moiré. RIGHT: Promenade dress of chamois-colored faille française, brocaded foulard of the same shade, and moss green velvet. The front of the skirt is of faille made in very fine vertical pleats; matching plastron is pleated in the same fashion. The corsage, open over this plastron, is, as is the tunic, made of brocaded foulard. This tunic, open over the skirt, is trimmed on either side by a wide revers in moss velvet tapering to a point at the hem. Corsage and sleeves trimmed with the same revers. A wide faille sash is draped around the waist and falls in front in two long tails.

No. 9. Toilettes de Mme. Delaunay, rue Godot de Mauroy, 49. (February 28)

LEFT: Short costume of wool and velvet in shaded sapphire color. Little spring mantelet of sapphire wool, shaped like a pelerine, ending in back at the waist in three loops. This pelerine is trimmed with a flat hood, lined in velvet, and framed by beaded passementerie in the same color; the center of the hood interior is adorned with an appliqué that matches the border; an ornament of the same passementerie on each shoulder. RIGHT: Short costume of plain brick red levantine and velvet-striped levantine in three shades of brick. Skirt composed of breadths of plain levantine alternating with panels of striped levantine, simulating a lower skirt placed under the levantine skirt, whose breadths appear to be buttoned onto the striped levantine. Demi-tunic of striped levantine draped in front and on the sides. Plain levantine jacket with striped revers. Striped plastron-corselet, completed by a guimpe of smooth crepe tied in a cravat; long sleeves with striped revers. Standing collar of solid-color brick velvet.

No. 10. Toilettes de Mme. Coussinet, rue Richer, 43. (March 7)

LEFT: Spring toilette of floral printed gaze pékinée of alternating ivy velvet and warp-printed gauze stripes. The front of the princesse dress is lightly draped. A wide ivy velvet bretelle falls from each side to the hem, where it ends in a point. A second band of the same velvet starts from the side of the corsage and descends parallel to the first. Between the two bands are three unbleached lace flounces long enough to cover the dress. RIGHT: Promenade toilette of walnut-colored Richelieu guipure, brocaded in red. The lower skirt is covered with a very wide gathered flounce. The polonaise, of the same goods, is caught up at the side, draped in back and buttoned on the bias. The hem is trimmed with a wide walnut velvet band. The corner of the side, raised in a polonaise and passed through a coulant, is faced with walnut velvet. Sleeve revers and a single corsage revers of the same velvet.

No. 11. Toilettes de Mme. Gradoz, rue de Provence, 52. (March 14)

LEFT: Dress of deep blue faille and golden brown cobweb toile. Peasant skirt of faille, open over the front of a toile skirt with matching wide revers ending in a point. Pointed corsage of toile with little open Spanish jacket of faille, tied only at the middle of the bust. Tight sleeves with toile revers. RIGHT: Dress of moss green aloe cloth. The skirt is open on the side with a garniture of two revers of deep red velvet with stripes of a lighter red. Under this opening, from top to bottom, is a breadth of pleated moss green faille. Pointed corsage with revers matching those of the skirt. Laced plastron, the bottom half plain and the top half pleat-

ed, with collar and sleeve revers of the velvet. The raised side of the skirt is held by two metal hooks with an antique silver finish. Rather tight sleeves, somewhat long and gathered.

No. 12. Toilettes de Mme. Coussinet, rue Richer, 43. (March 21)

LEFT: Toilette for a young woman of flowered pink bengaline with ivy-colored foliage, and ivy velvet. The skirt, draped in front, straight in back, opens on the left over an inset of pink gauze embroidered with ivy-colored beads and passementerie motifs. Corsage of ivy velvet, belted, opening over a gauze plastron matching the inset. Around the neckline, a cream smooth crepe fichu extends down the front and passes under the corsage, ending in shell-pleated cream lace. RIGHT: Dress of plain tussor foulard and the same foulard printed with flowers. Skirt of plain tussor, draped front and back. The sides are composed of printed tussor panels lined with garnet surah, draped at the top to form wide pleats toward the pouf. Pointed corsage with open neckline. The front is trimmed with three bows of garnet ribbon. The same bows ascend the side of the dress. The sleeves are stopped at the elbow by a garter of garnet ribbon ending in a bow.

No. 13. Toilettes de Mme. Gradoz, rue de Provence, 52. (March 28)

LEFT: Robe Colbert of larkspur silk grosgrain. The hem is trimmed with a heavy, pinked ruche. Corsage and skirt of spiderweb toile in a deeper shade of the same color, cut at the hem in a dentellated edge, repeating the bottom of the corsage. The corsage opens over a chemisette that matches the skirt; the latter is open in front revealing a breadth of the skirt covered with masses of ribbons. The fronts of the corsage and the skirt are trimmed with flat pieces of somewhat heavy white lace recalling Colbert lace. RIGHT: Costume of gold and blue glacé silk and old Flemish laces. The lower skirt is covered with these laces dipped in dye and tinted gold. The second skirt, of glacé silk, opens in front and is draped in the back, falling completely straight without trim. The corsage with frogged closing opens in a square over a chemisette of the same lace that trims the lower skirt. These laces form a kind of bouffant at the shoulder as well as toward the cuffs.

14. Toilettes de Mme. Coussinet, rue Richer, 43. (April 4)

LEFT: Visiting toilette. The first skirt, of changeable glacé surah in a pinkish copper shade, is trimmed with three insertions embroidered with colors to go with the surah. The draped tunic is made of a fancy openwork brocatelle, lined in surah. This tunic, caught up on the side, is turned back to show the lining. The corsage, of glacé surah, is cut in square flaps of varied lengths, edged with the same embroidered insertions as on the skirt. The corsage opens to reveal a very light, unglazed surah chemisette. RIGHT: Toilette for the races of embroidered net in a "creosote" (blackish brown) shade over pale Sèvres blue silk toile. The skirt is made of net, draped from top to bottom. This skirt begins at the left shoulder, leaves the right side of the corsage uncovered, and separates at the silk-gauze skirt which is covered with rosettes of ribbon of the same color as the gauze, where it is held with an inset. The sleeves are covered with the net. Round straw hat in creosote, trimmed with ribbon bows of creosote and pale blue arranged to form an aigrette.

No. 15. Chapeaux de Mlle. Boitte, 4, rue d'Alger. (April 11)

SUMMER HATS. UPPER LEFT: Hat without strings. Black lace, bordered with a half-wreath of roses without leaves, veiled with black lace. The same roses are arranged in an aigrette with a ruche of black lace. UPPER RIGHT: Round hat. Chestnut straw, white straw brim faced with chestnut velvet. The front is trimmed with snowballs. The back is covered with a garniture of chestnut ribbons. CENTER: Hat for a little girl. Black straw with a rolled brim trimmed with black velvet. The garniture is composed of red ribbons. Bunches of cherries hang down from the rather high, pointed crown. LOWER LEFT: Bonnet for an elderly lady of black lace with a diadem brim with gold bead embroidery and a thick cluster of white lilacs. LOWER RIGHT: Bonnet made with a netting of pearls in several sizes, edged with a wreath of satin and plush leaves. Atop the bonnet, two large blooming roses are held by a ribbon bow of moss green velvet.

No. 16. Toilettes de Mme. Gradoz, rue de Provence, 52. (April 18)

TOWN TOILETTES. LEFT: The bottom of the skirt of faille française in "reindeer antlers color" (light brown), is covered by a round skirt of bayadère openwork, with raised horizontal stripes. The tunic is made of plain faille française. Sash and bows, revers, corsage bands, and sleeve bands of velvet. The corsage opens over a guimpe of vertically pleated red surah. Round straw hat of string color, trimmed and lined with velvet. RIGHT: Skirt of figured cashmere. Overdress of plain pale blue cashmere edged at the hem and at the side openings by a band of the same goods as the skirt. The corsage of this dress, pleated à la grecque, is finished with a flat guimpe of the same stuff as the lower skirt. Undersleeves match the guimpe. Hanging sleeves, slit to the shoulder, of pale blue cashmere to match the dress. Belt of figured cashmere fastens under the arms with an openwork silver buckle. The pale blue cashmere skirt is pleated all around.

No. 17. Toilettes de Mme. Delaunay, rue Godot de Mauroy, 49. (April 25)

LEFT: Dinner toilette for a young woman. First skirt of wheat-colored faille, with otter-colored velvet zigzags 2 cm. (about ¾") wide. The tablier is covered with embroidery of chenille and otter-colored beads. The plastron of the décolleté corsage, matching the tablier, extends to the shoulders in such a way that only the sides and the back are of the same goods as the skirt. The corsage is bordered with a row of large otter-colored beads. RIGHT: Dinner toilette of pale blue satin and white point d'esprit. The first skirt, of pale blue faille, is covered with satin on which the net is draped at intervals with the help of satin ribbon bows. The tunic, of the same net, is edged with silver fringe. A sash of pale blue satin, edged with silver fringe, is draped on the tunic; sprays of roses spill over the sash. Corsage of draped net, with tiny décolleté jacket of pale blue satin, adorned with a cordon of roses. Very short point d'esprit sleeves.

No. 18. Toilettes de Mme. Coussinet, rue Richer, 43. (May 2)

LEFT: Spring toilette of doe-colored faille française. The pleated skirt, composed of two breadths of faille, opens widely over two draperies crossing in front made of ecru silk toile in a floral pattern. A drapery of the same toile passes between the two breadths of faille. The corsage of faille, is pointed, wide open in front, and adorned with floral embroidery. There are double pockets on each side, trimmed with the same embroidery. Doe-colored straw hat, trimmed with poppies. RIGHT: Toilette for the races of bordeaux-colored mosaic canvas, and striped foulard of the same shade. The front of the skirt is made of gathered foulard. A ribbon is threaded through a channel 20 cm. (about 8") above the hem. Plastron matching the skirt front and gathered in the same fashion; the corsage opening over the plastron, as well as the flat pleats that trim the sides of the skirt, are made of mosaic canvas; the pouf, like the sleeves, is embroidered with matching beads.

No. 19. Color plate missing from original book.

No. 20. Toilettes de Mme. Coussinet, rue Richer, 43. (May 16)

LEFT: Promenade toilette of canard blue and flame-colored changeable glacé surah. Skirt of pleated cream-color lace, crossed by wide horizontal canard blue ribbons. Polonaise of glacé surah, very draped on one side, falling straight on the other, raised in stepped pleats; the corsage has a draped plastron, with canard blue double revers on one side only; the half-length sleeves have pleated blue revers. A sash of the same color passes in front, then under the right side of the polonaise, to form a rather voluminous pouf in the rear. Canard-blue straw hat trimmed with double poppies. RIGHT: Toilette for the races of crepe etamine in cream and "serpent" color (gray blue green). Flat skirt in serpent color with horizontal stripes in cream. Polonaise draped on one side,

arranged in a pointed panier with embroidery at the corner; the other side falling in straight pleats edged with a band of braid matching the stripes and arranged in loops. The front of the polonaise is adorned, from shoulder to waist, with the same band, and opens over a shirred chemisette of cream crepe.

No. 21. Toilettes de Mme. Gradoz, rue de Provence, 52. (May 23)

LEFT: Toilette for visiting or the races. Lower skirt of wild cherry silk covered with Richelieu lace. Pardessus-redingote of blue faille shot with rainbow stripes, revealing the entire front of the skirt and held by twisted braid "of a thousand knots;" the same ornament on the corsage and the sleeves. A small fichu of Richelieu lace adorns the upper part of the corsage. The pardessus is also open in back over the pouf. Long, plain sleeves. RIGHT: Dress of cream etamine, embroidered with tiny pompadour bouquets, and red and blue glacé surah. The skirt, made of surah, trimmed at the hem with a little ruffle of large piping, is covered with three etamine skirts superimposed on each other, scalloped in color at the hem. Crossed surah corsage attached to a drapery short in front, very long in back. A fichu of etamine trims the corsage. Half-length sleeves. The drapery of the skirt is pleated on both hips, then behind, where, almost as long as the lower skirt, it falls in large pleats.

No. 22. Toilettes d'Enfants des Grands Magasins du Louvre. (May 30)

FROM LEFT TO RIGHT: *Five-year-old girl.* Robe anglaise of sky blue mousseline de laine. The hem is trimmed with a flat band of embroidered nainsook. Pleated plastron is surrounded by bands arranged as bretelles. Sky blue faille belt stops at either side of the plastron, where it is trimmed with bunches of narrow ribbons to match the belt. A matching bow is at the left side of the neckline. White straw hat with a white ostrich plume. *Eighteen-month-old boy.* Turkey red dress with a yoke and large pleats, trimmed at the hem, the neckline, and the sleeves with white bands embroidered in red. *Three-year-old girl.* Low-necked dress of white nainsook completely embroidered in navy blue cotton. Navy blue sash tied in a bow on the side. *Four-year-old boy.* Sailor suit of navy blue jersey with red cuffs and trimming. *Ten- or eleven-year-old girl.* Robe anglaise of bronze wool. Pardessus with large square pockets opens over a bouffant plastron made of surah in a lighter shade of the same color, held by a belt. Hat of bronze and yellow straw trimmed and lined in red. *Five-year-old boy.* Knickers and peasant jacket of golden brown wool. The jacket is open over a bouffant chemisette of cream wool. Cream cravat with a large bow. *Six-year-old girl.* Cream batiste dress trimmed with two bands of embroidery. Plastron framed by two narrower bands. Sash, neck bow, and hair bow of pink ribbon. *Eight-year-old girl.* Beige wool checked dress. Braid trimmed with tiny balls simulates a hood. On the hips, a twisted cord ending in tassels ties on the side.

No. 23. Toilettes de Mme. Coussinet, rue Richer, 43. (June 6)

CASINO TOILETTES. LEFT: Lower skirt of azure faille, covered with a deep cream lace flounce. On each side there is a silk-and-wool panel, with bayadère stripes of cream and azure; long barège drapery in front and back. Corsage of bayadère with collar and cuffs of blue faille, open over a guimpe of pleated mousseline. Round straw hat trimmed with cornflowers and wheat. RIGHT: Dress of old rose silk mousseline and pompadour foulard with stripes of the same shade. The mousseline de soie skirt is arranged in front in very fine pleats. They are held in 30 cm. (about 12") above the hem by a channel threaded with pink ribbon with a bow at the side. The Louis XV corsage-jacket is made of pompadour foulard; a quille and a scalloped drapery of the same foulard trim the left side and the back of the skirt; this drapery is held by wide rosettes of pink ribbon.

No. 24. Toilettes de Mme. Gradoz, rue de Provence, 52. (June 13)

LEFT: Costume of batiste-zephyr in plain blue and blue striped with red. The pleated skirt is striped. The tunic, completely open, is composed of a pouf and breadths falling straight, and made, like the jacket, of plain batiste. The jacket is open over a pleated striped chemisette. The jacket, with falling collar embroidered in red, is trimmed with large buttons of pearly cat's eye. Red ribbon sash passes under the jacket and ties in back. Above the large collar there is a tiny red velvet collar. RIGHT: Dress of very sheer embroidered ecru lawn over an underskirt of very pale blue faille. Ecru lawn covers the skirt. The corsage and the draped dress are made of solid-color ecru lawn. The corsage, lined in faille to match the skirt, is trimmed with wide revers of the faille, richly embroidered. At the hip, a sash of wide and supple ribbon in ecru and blue bayadère stripes, ties on the side and falls in two long, fringed tails. The half-length sleeves are trimmed with embroidered pale blue faille revers.

No. 25. Toilettes de Mme. Coussinet, rue Richer, 43. (June 20)

LEFT: Promenade dress of copper China grenadine with cream-colored flowers and plain grenadine. The pleated skirt is attached on one side to a very deep ecru lace flounce that covers the front and part of the other side of the dress. Tunic in two shawl points and pouf of solid grenadine. The cuirasse corsage of flowered grenadine is cut and crossed toward the armholes, leaving only the height of a corselet under the arms; it is completed by a high-necked gathered chemisette of plain copper grenadine with standing collar and cuffs of copper velvet. A cluster composed of several long looped rosettes of solid-copper ribbon falls between the two points of the tunic. Round straw hat of ecru straw, lined with copper velvet, trimmed with a bird in several shades of copper. RIGHT: Toilette for the races of ivory openwork goods, striped in cashmere. The skirt, of this stuff, is cut in large square dentellations at the hem, revealing bands of ivory wool lace. All this rests on a skirt of ivory silk. Serving as a corsage, a little jacket of the same striped goods, in the shape of a habit in back, opens in front and is finished by a solid color openwork drapery. Rather short sleeves, with deep revers. Hat of ivory straw, lined in pale-blue velvet, trimmed with a mixture of pale blue and shrimp pink gauze.

No. 26. Toilettes de Mme. Gradoz, rue de Provence, 52. (June 27)

LEFT: Navy blue etamine skirt, embroidered with tiny dark red flowers, open at the side with red faille revers joined by three red bows. Under this skirt, scalloped in red at the hem, there is an etamine skirt of the same color, not embroidered, and pleated all around, over a foundation of red foulard. Pleated corsage of embroidered etamine adorned with red revers, open over a solid etamine plastron. Red ribbon collar with bow. Half-length sleeves with red cuffs. Hat of grayish brown straw lined in navy blue faille, trimmed with poppies. RIGHT: Dress of sea green surah covered with Saxony lace held by a rosette-bow of ruby velvet. Polonaise of the surah is fastened at the side and adorned with a Saxony lace drapery caught up at intervals by ruby rosettes. The corsage opens over a guimpe of pleated white muslin, and the neckline is bordered with a standing collar lined in ruby velvet. Half-length sleeves slashed over a puff of lace trimmed with ruby rosettes. Latticework straw hat, bordered and trimmed with ruby poppies.

No. 27. Toilettes de Mme. Delaunay, rue Godot de Mauroy, 49. (July 4)

LEFT: Toilette of cream leze orientale embroidered in red and blue. The first skirt of batiste or silk is trimmed with two leze flounces; the tunic is of leze, very long, draped in back and raised on the left hip under a bow of red ribbon; open pointed corsage, completed by a draped fichu of plain lawn; rather full half-length sleeves, gathered into a somewhat full cuff; the lawn sleeves are trimmed with a band of leze. RIGHT: Toilette of cotton crepon and matching lace. The lower skirt (of batiste or taffeta) is covered with crepon flounces with the same drapery in back; in front, a tunic, similar in shape, is attached by ribbon bows; the side breadth of the skirt, of the crepon, is pleated and trimmed with lace arranged in chevrons. The corsage, of crepon, is open over a pleated plastron framed in lace; on the shoulders, ribbon bows; half-length sleeves, adorned with lace and ribbon.

No. 28. Toilettes de Mme. Coussinet, rue Richer, 43. (July 11)

LEFT: Toilette for the races. Ivory foulard with Persian pattern in old-rose and "amadou" (deep garnet). The skirt, pleated vertically on the right side, is raised slightly on the other side; its hem is decorated with a deep band with a printed Persian pattern in amadou and old rose. A very short jacket of the foulard serves as a corsage, gathered on one side at the shoulder and held by a bow. The jacket is outlined with a band like the skirt, but narrower. The jacket is worn over a pointed velvet corselet of amadou velvet. RIGHT: Seaside toilette of faience blue crepe. First round skirt is pleated vertically with multicolored threads arranged in a Scottish plaid. A long tunic with paniers, made of the same plain crepe, crosses in front at the waist, opening wide over the skirt front, ending in a point at each side and draped in back. As a corsage, a little jacket of bordeaux velvet opening over a smooth white crepe chemisette which finishes a plastron of faience blue crepe. From the top to the bottom of this opening, the jacket is joined by bordeaux velvet chevrons. Hat of coarse golden-brown straw, lined with bordeaux velvet.

No. 29. Toilettes de Mme. Gradoz, rue de Provence, 52. (July 18)

LEFT: Costume of striped ecru etamine and lynx-colored velvet. A drapery of striped etamine opens on the side to reveal a fan-pleated skirt of ecru surah. Lynx velvet tabs cross over the fan pleats and are joined by a large fancy button. The corsage, made of striped etamine, is decorated with bretelles of lynx velvet joined by crossed tabs of the velvet. Long sleeves with velvet revers. RIGHT: Skirt of "dragonfly-colored" (light blue) surah, gathered around the waist, held in 20 cm. (about 8") above the hem by a thick ruche of the surah. Corsage and skirt back (stopping at each side behind the arms) of brocaded Pompadour on a moss-green ground with multicolored flowers. This half-skirt, pleated at the waist, falls completely straight. The pointed corsage opens over a plastron of plissé surah like the skirt. Corsage revers, horizontal bands across the plastron, collar and sleeve revers are of dragonfly velvet.

No. 30. Toilettes de Mme. Coussinet, rue Richer, 43. (July 25)

LEFT: Toilette for the casino and summer visits. Crepon with red and blue stripes on an ecru ground and antique blue pongee. Skirt of crepon gathered to a flat yoke 25 cm. (about 10") deep. Corselet with shoulder straps, of pongee; laces in front with the help of a rather wide matching ribbon. The corselet is completed by a guimpe with a high-necked yoke and half-length sleeves. Band collar and cuffs of pongee. In the back, two somewhat long breadths of pongee are draped in a pouf. Hat of ecru straw faced in antique blue and adorned with an antique blue feather. RIGHT: Seaside toilette. Scotch plaid wool toile in "tripoli" (light red) and billiard green. Skirt of plain tripoli, arranged in front in flat, vertical pleats. Polonaise is the same length as the skirt, very pleated at the waist, mounting to a yoke at the neck. This yoke is made of billiard green moiré. Moiré sleeve revers and wide hip sash. Red beret.

No. 31. Toilettes de Mme. Gradoz, rue de Provence, 52. (August 1)

LEFT: Seaside toilette of solid cream-color pongee and the same pongee patterned with dahlias. The skirt, of the patterned goods, dagged at the hem, falls over a wide dahlia-colored velvet edging. Open polonaise crossing in front over a small plastron of the same velvet, is rather long in back, forming two unequal paniers on the sides, one ending in a point, the other rounded, dagged at its edge and trimmed with a narrower edging of dahlia velvet than the skirt. The polonaise, like the corsage, is of plain pongee, with a plissé fichu and sleeve revers of patterned pongee. Hat of gilded straw, lined with dahlia velvet and trimmed with little dahlias. RIGHT: Toilette of surah and faille française in serpent blue. The skirt is covered with two deep surah flounces, dagged at the hem and embroidered; the back falls over a faille skirt. A little faille tunic falls from each side under the arms in a long panel ending in fringe. Pouf and corsage of surah. The corsage opens over a faille plastron, embroidered over its entire surface.

32. (August 8)

LEFT: Casino toilette. Pale mauve crepe de chine and deep mauve velvet. Pale mauve taffeta covered with two deep gathered flounces of cream silk lace. Corselet with shoulder straps of mauve velvet, very low square neckline, over a little plissé guimpe of the crepe de chine. Two paniers of the crepe are taken below the corsage and draped in such a fashion as to form a point at either side of the corselet, then open over the skirt. Shepherdess hat of ecru straw, trimmed with mauve mallows. The tunic forms a pouf in back. The sleeves of the corselet are of crepe de chine and end at the elbow where they are held by a band of velvet to match the corselet. RIGHT: Dress of canvas cloth, patterned with an Oriental design mixed with gold. Round skirt with similar tunic, raised at the left hip, forming a point in front and a pouf in back. The raised side of the tunic is bordered with a ruby velvet ribbon which passes through tiny loops, ending in a cluster of ribbon rosettes. On the raised side, another cluster, and two long tails of the same ribbon. Belted corsage gathered in front, laced with a narrow ribbon of ruby velvet. Velvet belt. On each shoulder, a cluster of ruby ribbons. Standing collar of the velvet.

No. 33. Toilettes de Mme. Delaunay, rue Godot de Mauroy, 49. (August 15)

LEFT: Short costume of sandalwood-color bengaline and striped faille française. The first skirt, of lightweight taffeta, is covered at the hem in bias-striped faille. The second skirt, of bengaline, is pleated in large fluting; its hem is decorated with bead embroidery. This second skirt is completed in back by a faille drapery, which extends on the sides in a little panier. High-necked faille corsage, open over a gilet. The fronts of the corsage are adorned with bead embroidery; beaded epaulettes; the hem of the corsage ends in little basques. Hat of straw to match the dress, trimmed with brown velvet. RIGHT: Toilette of Louis XV lilac faille française and ecru net with raised embroidery. The skirt is covered with the net; dress of the faille, draped in back, raised on the side. The open corsage, bordered with net, crosses at the side under ribbons with streamers; the faille sleeves, covered in net, are worn somewhat nonchalantly; under the plain corsage, a plissé guimpe of white muslin, with faille collar covered with the net. Hat of straw lined in velvet to match the dress, trimmed with white doves.

No. 34. Toilettes de Mme. Gradoz, rue de Provence, 52. (August 22)

LEFT: Costume of pongee striped in several shades of garnet, garnet surah, and garnet velvet. The skirt, made of the pongee, is decorated 20 cm. (about 8") above the hem by a row of bows in several shades of garnet. Draped tunic of surah, raised on one side and lined in pongee. Velvet corselet with shoulder straps, edged with small ball fringes. The same edging on the tunic. Chemisette and sleeves of the corselet are of pongee. Round hat of ecru straw, faced in garnet velvet. RIGHT: Costume of cream-colored crepon and French blue velvet embroidered with blue-tinted pearls. The skirt, of crepon, is covered with five flounces. The top part, arranged like a Moliere shirt, puffs out and falls over the point of the blue velvet peplum. Two equal points fall on the sides. All three end in a triple tassel. The corsage is a fitted jacket of the same velvet, ending in three points in front, square basques on either side, and in a little point in back. This sleeveless jacket is open in front over a plissé crepon chemisette. Plissé crepon sleeves with velvet sleeve bands embroidered in pearls like the outline of the corsage.

No. 35. Toilettes de Mme. Coussinet, rue Richer, 43. (August 29)

LEFT: Chateau toilette of cream openwork grenadine over Sèvres blue grenadine. Pleated skirt draped in back; in the center of the skirt is a wide pleat of plain cream etamine embroidered with flowers of Sèvres blue and old red. The pleated corsage opens over an etamine plastron embroidered to match the skirt; on either side of the front skirt pleat there is a drapery trimmed with cream lace, held at each hip by a beaded passementerie cluster. The corsage is adorned with a wide collar. RIGHT: Promenade toilette of terra-cotta silk toile, patterned and plain. The pleated skirt

is composed of alternating patterned and plain panels. Two very short draperies forming crossed paniers adorn the top of the skirt and form a pouf bow in back. Pointed corsage pleated on the shoulders with a single revers and collar of terra-cotta velvet. Half-length sleeves with velvet revers.

No. 36. Toilettes de Mme. Gradoz, rue de Provence, 52. (September 5)

LEFT: Costume of navy blue bengaline and velvet striped with gold thread and otter on the same blue. The center of the skirt, of bengaline, is fan-pleated. The rest of the skirt is velvet. The bengaline tunic opens over the skirt; slightly draped at the sides, it falls in two long tails in back which cover the velvet skirt. The corsage is velvet; it opens over a velvet plastron with bengaline revers and is completed by a bengaline gilet. Bengaline sleeves with velvet cuffs. RIGHT: Louis XIII costume for promenades and visiting. Skirt of terra-cotta vigognette. The front pleat is 40 cm. (about 16") wide and is covered with strips of vigognette placed horizontally, ending in a triangle at each side where they are attached by buttons of burnished steel. The rest of the skirt is pleated; each pleat is 12 cm. (about 5") wide. A small scarf of the same goods passes in front and is tied in back in a large bow. Gilet covered with strips of braid and held by a belt with a burnished steel buckle. Little matching jacket, opening over a plissé plastron. The jacket is made with rather long basques, slit on the side.

No. 37. Toilettes de Mme. Coussinet, rue Richer, 43. (September 12)

LEFT: Costume of figured surah striped in wood brown and ecru. The entire garment is cut on the bias. The skirt is pleated vertically. The matching tunic is draped on the sides and back. The skirt is open on the side over an inset of brown velvet. The drapery of the tunic is held by a cluster of brown ribbon rosettes. Brown velvet gilet. Jacket of striped surah, fitted in back, gathered in front, open over the gilet. Collar and cuffs of brown velvet. RIGHT: Skirt of surah ecossais. Pleated all around, raised on one side and pleated to reveal an olive-green lining. Under the raised side is an underskirt of the same goods. Blue-green cashmere skirt, draped in back, raised on the sides and pleated in front. Matching short corsage, open front and back over a chemisette which matches the skirt. The corsage is trimmed front and back with wide surah revers. Surah cuffs. Ending the corsage are basques of the surah.

No. 38. Toilettes de Mme. Gradoz, rue de Provence, 52. (September 19)

HUNTING COSTUMES. LEFT: Short skirt, entirely pleated, made of ribbed gray velvet, open on the side to reveal an inset of brown kid. The skirt appears to button onto the inset with big steel buttons. Jacket-corsage with diagonal closing has the same big buttons. The corsage has a basque on the right side; the left is rounded like a Figaro jacket, ending at a kidskin gilet that matches the inset. The game bag falls on the right side. Round hat with brim-visor, of brown silk felt with a brown bird. RIGHT: Short skirt covered at the hem and the side with suede. Tunic of suede-colored lightweight wool. Long suede gilet with pockets. Short jacket of the same wool as the tunic, with suede revers that open over a colored striped toile chemisette. Red cravat tied à la Colin. Silk felt hat in suede color, with three feathers attached by a steel buckle.

No. 39. Toilettes de Mme. Coussinet, rue Richer, 43. (September 26)

LEFT: Visiting dress of ochre-colored faille française and moiré. The first skirt and the plastron are moiré. The tunic is faille, open in front, draped toward the waist, passing over the left hip and ending on the pouf in a scarf. The plain corsage, open over the plastron, is edged with bead embroidery. On the right side of the corsage there is a completely embroidered basque. The same embroidery around the edge of the tunic and on the epaulets. Velvet collar. RIGHT: Traveling toilette. Scotch-plaid cashmere in cream, blue, and green, with red and yellow threads. The skirt, very draped around the waist, is raised on the left side by a long buttoned tab. The fitted jacket reveals a cream piqué gilet at the neck and waist. The jacket, piped in red velvet, has a red velvet collar and revers. All the buttons are covered in red velvet. Round hat of sand-color braided silk, lined in red velvet.

No. 40. Toilettes de Mme. Delaunay, rue Godot de Mauroy, 49. (October 3)

LEFT: Dress of double-faced faille française in two shades of iron gray. Skirt, of the darker shade, is arranged in wide pleats facing in one direction. Each pleat is edged with a strip of ombred gray feathers, piped on each side with a line of flame feathers. The same trim is on the hem. Draped faille tunic in the lighter shade, raised at the hip with a bow of faille ribbon in both shades. The pointed corsage, in the deeper tone, is trimmed with light-colored drapery and edged with a strip of feathers. The sleeves have the same trim. RIGHT: Costume of deep checked etamine and dark red velvet. The velvet skirt is arranged in wide pleats. Tunic with three tails is of etamine. The front tail, plissé, ends in a large velvet bow by which it is attached to the skirt; the other two puff out a little to form paniers. On either side tail, a large velvet bow without tails. An etamine drapery descends in back. Pointed corsage with velvet sleeves. The corsage, high-necked, lined in velvet, is open over a high-necked chemisette made of dark red crepe anglais. An etamine ruche edges the sleeve.

No. 41. Chapeaux de Mme. Boitte, 4, rue d'Alger. (October 10)

WINTER HATS. UPPER LEFT: Phrygian bonnet of gray plissé velours. The rolled edge, of the same velvet, is covered with bead embroidery in several shades of gray. A curled feather of the same color, attached at the back edge, is drawn over the top of the hat. The tip of the feather adorns the front of the hat. UPPER RIGHT: Tall toque of black silk felt. Edge of red plush. The garniture is composed of a red bird feather and four black silk pompons. CENTER: Round hat of black velvet with rather wide brim, narrowed and raised on one side. It is trimmed in back with wide rosettes of black satin ribbon. In front, a sulphur feather laid flat; in back, the same feather, curved. LOWER LEFT: Bonnet Marguerite of Burgundy, made entirely of tiny peacock feathers, with a rolled edging of peacock blue velvet. This bonnet, which is very close in shape to a coif, consists of two pieces joined by a ground of pale antique gold satin. In front, a bird of the same tone as the ground. Narrow peacock blue velvet strings attached close to the ear by a piece of costume jewelry. LOWER RIGHT: Hat with forward brim of golden brown satin covered with gold lace. The brim is lined in brown velvet. The high crown is adorned with feathers in shades of gold. Strings of golden brown satin are tied under the chin.

No. 42. Toilettes de Mme. Gradoz, rue de Provence, 52. (October 17)

LEFT: Toilette for visiting and little dinners, of antique-style wool with hazelnut pattern on a bronze green ground and bronze bengaline. Bengaline skirt arranged in fan-shape in front, framed by revers of the wool. The back of the skirt is pleated vertically. Demi-paniers of bengaline sit on the revers. The corsage, of wool, is pointed in front, two large pleated tails descending to the hem in back. The top of the demi-décolleté corsage is open over a plissé bengaline guimpe. The neckline, the sleeves, and the hem of the corsage are edged with little bouillonnés. A guimpe of lace or white India muslin may be substituted for the guimpe of bengaline, which is removable. RIGHT: Costume of star cloth in "reindeer antlers" (light brown) and otter. The solid-color skirt is adorned with several otter velvet ribbons. The skirt, draped in back, is trimmed in front with two pleated revers ending in a band of otter velvet. Corsage of the same cloth with plastron striped with otter velvet. A single revers, collar, and sleeve trim of otter velvet.

No. 43. Toilettes de Mme. Coussinet, rue Richer, 43. (October 24)

LEFT: Toilette for visiting and promenades in plush and epingline in "dead leaf" color (brown). The plush has wide stripes on an ivory satin ground, covered with a pattern in cashmere blue and dead leaf. The lower skirt, flat in front, is adorned with a band of the plush ending in a fringe of silk and beads. The corsage and the draperies are of plain epingline. The corsage, in the shape of a polonaise, is trimmed with two plush insets. The same plush is on the front of the corsage. RIGHT: Promenade toilette of faille française and epingle velvet in cloud gray. The skirt, of epingle velvet with horizontal cisele stripes, is entirely flat. The polonaise, of the faille, buttons on the side like the corsage. It is raised at the sides. On the left side there is a simulated pocket made of gray pearl buttons in a darker shade than the goods. The sleeve, open at the top, is trimmed with velvet slashing and adorned with the same buttons as on the skirt and the front of the corsage. Collar and cuffs of the velvet.

No. 44. Toilettes de Mme. Gradoz, rue de Provence, 52. (October 31)

LEFT: At-home toilette. Bouclé and vigogne in otter color. The front of the bouclé skirt consists of pleats, broken by vertical round pleats of plain vigogne. The hem of the skirt front is trimmed with a torsade fringe of silk and chenille. The polonaise-blouse, of plain vigogne, heavily draped over the hips, opens over a Russian shirt of crimson velvet, held by a broad belt of otter and gold. Collar and sleeve revers (funnel-shaped) of bouclé, with lining of crimson velvet. RIGHT: Costume of gray sicilienne with narrow strips of dark gray braid. Round dress trimmed with strips of braid. Tunic, almost as long as the skirt, is decoupé on its edges in rather wide curves adorned with three gray galons. The tunic is slit on the side from top to bottom and joined by three somewhat large bows of gray reps ribbon. The high-necked corsage with slightly long basques is decoupé on all its edges. The fronts are joined by four ribbon bows over a fitted gilet of the same sicilienne. Round hat of gray felt, faced with garnet velvet and trimmed with feathers shaded from garnet to pink.

No. 45. Toilettes de Mme. Coussinet, rue Richer, 43. (November 7)

LEFT: Pleated underskirt of Scotch plaid pout-de-soie in garnet, tobacco, gold, and moss. The redingote is made of deep blue thibet. This redingote, with crossed corsage, is open wide on the left side to reveal a large part of the underskirt, on which extremely big buttons attach the large revers of the redingote; the other side of the redingote is doubled back on itself to form another large revers also buttoned on the skirt. Under the crossed corsage, near the neck, there is a tiny garnet plastron. RIGHT: Visiting toilette. Skirt of ivy-colored faille française. The front, pleated vertically, is trimmed with a little draped tunic. The corsage-jacket is made of silky velvet striped in ivy on a shrimp ground. A panel of the stripe trims the side of the skirt and is joined in front by a passementerie inset beaded in shrimp and ivy. The inside of the jacket consists of a drapery in shrimp surah. Between the two skirt fronts and ending in a point, there is the same motif as the passementerie inset. Elbow-length sleeves.

No. 46. Toilettes d'Enfants des Grands Magasins du Louvre. (November 14)

FROM LEFT TO RIGHT: *Twelve-year-old girl.* Redingote of sand-color vigogne, gathered around the neck and down the front. The plastron, also gathered, is framed by sand-color plush revers joined at the waist by a metal hook. Collar of the same plush. Toque of otter plush edged with fur, with a blue bird on the side. *Seven-year-old girl.* Russian blouse of black velvet, composed of a pleated skirt and a sleeveless corsage, wide open with a yoke. Plissé blouse and long sleeves of red surah. *Eight-year-old boy.* Knickers and pleated jacket of medium gray cloth. *Ten-year-old girl.* Bronze wool dress. The skirt, pleated, is open at the side over red and white striped wool. Matching plastron. The corsage, open over this plastron, is trimmed with revers of the same stripe. *Thirteen-year-old girl.* Navy blue cloth skirt with flounce of the same color wool embroidered in vivid red silk. Jacket of the same cloth as the skirt, with red silk gilet opened wide over the chemisette. Soft sash, fringed in soft red silk. Hat of navy blue felt trimmed with red and navy blue birds. *Five-year-old girl.* Dress of tobacco plush with pleated skirt. The corsage is open front and back over a plissé corsage of cream surah. Sash of tobacco-color satin ribbon. *Six-year-old boy.* Sailor suit of medium blue cloth with red and white striped plastron. Large pale blue collar of wool mousseline.

No. 47. Toilettes de Mme. Gradoz, rue de Provence, 52. (November 21)

LEFT: Flat skirt of Scotch-plaid green and blue velvet. All the breadths are cut in points. Polonaise of dark blue sicilienne forms two long points in front and is arranged in several draperies in back. The corsage, with plaid revers to match the skirt, opens over a plastron of the same goods as the polonaise, horizontally plissé. RIGHT: Plain golden brown velvet skirt pleated vertically all around. Tunic of golden brown bengaline in a lighter shade than the skirt, trimmed with velvet ribbons to match the skirt. The tails of the tunic, raised à la washerwoman, are lined in satin the same color as the skirt. Corsage with very short basques and a diagonal closing, made of the same bengaline as the tunic and also trimmed with velvet ribbons. A half-collar like the corsage is placed on the wider side of the diagonal corsage. Round hat of deep golden brown plush, trimmed with feathers in several shades of golden brown.

No. 48. Toilettes de Mme. Coussinet, rue Richer, 43. (November 28)

LEFT: Promenade and visiting toilette of garnet sicilienne. The hem is decorated with a wide band of plaid velvet, in garnet and black. A short tunic of the sicilienne, very draped, adorns the side of the skirt and forms a pouf. On the side, an inset of plain garnet velvet ends in two points. The belted corsage opens over a plastron of plain velvet near the neck. The fronts are trimmed with a band of plaid velvet. Hat of garnet felt and plush. RIGHT: Visiting toilette of faille française embroidered in a lichen-color swirled pattern and oak-colored solid plush. The faille skirt is gathered at the waist and is open over a band of plush. The skirt is attached to the plush with large golden buttons. The corsage, short in front, forms a polonaise in back. The sides of the corsage descend in long tails trimmed with plush which narrow towards the bottom and end in a thick fringe. The corsage opens over a plain plush plastron with a matching collar. Bonnet of oak plush, with feathers shading toward apricot.

No. 49. Toilettes de Mme. Gradoz, rue de Provence, 62. (December 5)

LEFT: Bridal toilette. Underdress of white faille edged with a wide ruche of the same faille, covered with a white lace plissé skirt slightly draped at the side. Train of white faille with wide stripes. A sash of orange blossoms, attached on the side, falls over the lace skirt. High-necked, pointed corsage, open over a plastron of plissé white silk gauze. Headdress of orange blossoms and large veil of tulle illusion. RIGHT: Dress of amethyst faille. The skirt, plain all around, is pleated on the side. The pleats are adorned with staggered bands of matching plush. Tunic open on the side, very draped with a rear pouf. A band of plush arranged in rosettes with long streamers falls down the open side. High-necked, pointed corsage with plush yoke.

No. 50. Toilettes de Mme. Coussinet, rue Richer, 43. (November 12)

BALL GOWNS. LEFT: Toilette of maize novelty net over matching satin. The underdress, of satin, is trimmed with a pleated flounce adorned at intervals with bows of maize satin ribbon. The tunic, of the net, is draped on the side in fan-pleats held by a bow. Two satin ribbons are passed through both hems and mark the outline of the drapery raised on the side. The cuirasse corsage, of maize satin, is décolleté. It is garnished with a net drapery. In back, the pouf is trimmed with masses of satin ribbons. RIGHT: Evening toilette. Plain gauze and sky blue patterned gauze. The skirt is gathered at the waist and forms large pleats under the arms. Three ribbons pass over and under the pleats of the dress and end in a bow at the left. The right side of the skirt, very draped, connects the pouf of patterned gauze. The rest of the toilette is of plain gauze. The décolleté corsage is draped from top to bottom, and decorated with ribbon bows. The same bows on both shoulders.

No. 51. Toilettes de Mme. Delaunay, rue Godot de Mauroy, 49. (December 19)

LEFT: Plush skirt with stripes of "Byron color" (olive green) and "Olga" (Louis XV pink). The tunic, the corsage, and the sleeves are of plain Louis XV satin. The tunic, short on one side, is raised to hip level on the other, falling to the hem in back. The corsage is round at the waist, open over a plastron that matches the skirt and the bouillonné inset on the sleeves. RIGHT: Costume of pomponnette velvet and matching plain velvet. Lower skirt of faille covered with a skirt of pomponnette. Tunic of plain velvet. Corsage with plain velvet collar and revers open over a plastron of pomponnette velvet. The sleeves are rather wide, gathered vertically, ending in a velvet cuff.

No. 52. Toilettes de Mme. Coussinet, rue Richer, 43. (December 26)

LEFT: Visiting toilette. Tonkinoise in "Ganges-color" (a kind of tired blue). Plain skirt of plush and faille with very wide stripes of the same Ganges. Over this skirt, between openings, falls a skirt of tonkinoise. The pouf is separated from the skirt by a wide revers ending in a point, of the stripe. Pointed corsage with embroidered decoration. Small visite of black velvet with passementerie and beaded garniture. RIGHT: Dress of lizard green faille française. Skirt pleated on one side; second skirt as long as the first, draped on the opposite side, arranged in a pouf in back, open over the pleated side of the first skirt. Both sides of this opening are bordered with wide revers of old rose faille, covered with multicolor embroidery. The corsage, round at the waist, is plissé on one side; the other is adorned with a large sailor collar embroidered like the revers. The sleeves and a band on the hem of the underskirt are also embroidered. Round hat, in lizard green plush, trimmed with old rose feathers.

GLOSSARY

Aigrette: Upright tuft of feathers; something resembling a feather aigrette.

Aloe cloth: Cloth made of a hemp-like fiber of a fleshy-leaved century plant or similar plant.

Barège: Gauze-like fabric of silk, combined with wool.

Basque: Small peplum.

Batiste-zephyr: Lightweight, sheer cotton; any article made of very light material.

Bayadère: Crosswise multicolored stripes; fabric with such stripes.

Bengaline: Heavy-ribbed silk with a corded effect.

Bouillonnés: Shirred bands of fabric; puffs.

Bretelles: Shaped bands worn over the shoulders and attached in back and front to a waistband.

Brocatelle: Heavy figured fabric with a raised Jacquard pattern, higher than brocade.

Changeable: Fabric woven with a warp of one color and a weft of another giving different effects in varying light.

Chantilly: Type of bobbin lace.

Chemisette: A sleeveless vestee or dickey made of fine cotton, lace, or net, used primarily to fill low necklines.

Ciselé: Velvet with patterns created by leaving some of the loops formed to create the pile uncut.

Coif: Close-fitting cap.

Corsage: Bodice or upper part of woman's dress.

Corselet: Lightly boned corset.

Coulant: Ring or loop.

Crepe: Fabric with a grained or crinkled surface; can be made of silk, cotton, wool, etc.

Crepon: Fabric similar to crepe, but heavier and firmer; generally of silk or a mixture.

Cuirasse bodice or corsage: A bodice lined and boned to fit smoothly over the torso.

Dagged: Cut into points, leaves, or scallops along the edge.

Décolleté: Cut very low at the neckline.

Decoupé: Cut out.

Dentellated: Notched or scalloped.

Epaulet: Shoulder ornament.

Épinglé: Ribbed or corded fabric, usually silk.

Épingline: Ribbed dress fabric made with silk warp and wool filling.

Étamine: Light, loosely woven plain weave cotton or worsted fabric.

Faille française: Silk faille made in France.

Faille: Finely ribbed silk, cotton, or wool.

Fichu: Small triangular or rectangular shawl or scarf, usually of fine soft fabric, worn over the shoulders and generally tied in the front like a kerchief.

Foulard: Fine soft silk or cotton in a twill weave, often printed in a small design.

Galon: Narrow, tape-like band.

Garniture: Decorative trimming.

Gaze pékinée: Fabric with alternating velvet and gauze stripes.

Gilet: Sleeveless bodice with a decorative front.

Glacé silk: Silk with a smooth, highly polished surface.

Grenadine: Fine, gauze-like fabric of silk or silk and wool.

Grosgrain: Fabric or ribbon with heavy ribs.

Guimpe: Waist-length blouse, generally of sheer cotton, with short or long sleeves.

Guipure: Various large-patterned heavy laces, the motifs connected by brides instead of a net ground.

Illusion: Fine tulle net, usually silk.

Jaspé: Fabric woven with twisted yarns of varying shades, giving a streaked blending of colors.

Justaucorps: Close-fitting, long-skirted coat.

Levantine: Sturdy silk cloth with a twill weave.

Leze orientale: A machine-woven lace fabric.

Mantelet: Outer garment similar to a shawl made with some tailoring.

Moiré: Stiff, ribbed silk-and-cotton fabric with a watered effect.

Mosaic canvas: Fine silk or cotton canvas, used as a base for embroidery.

Mousseline de laine: Wool muslin, often printed.

Mousseline: Fine, soft muslin.

Nainsook: A thin, delicate, plain weave cotton.

Ombréd: Graduated in color.

Panier: A structure or device worn at the sides to extend the hips. Also, a portion of a skirt arranged to provide fullness at the sides.

Pantaloons: Trousers.

Pardessus: Literally, overcoat. A general term for outer garments in the nineteenth century.

Passementerie: Applied trimmings such as braid, cords, and heavy embroideries.

Pelerine: Cape or cloak of varying length.

Phrygian bonnet: Brimless cap.

Piqué: Firm fabric with a lengthwise corded effect.

Plastron: A V-shaped front of a woman's costume.

Plissé: Gathered or pleated.

Point d'esprit: Net or tulle with dots.

Polonaise: A coat-gown with the fronts of the skirts pulled back over an underskirt.

Pompadour: Small floral effect in soft shades.

Pongee: A lightweight, natural-colored textile, usually of silk with an irregular texture in a plain weave.

Pouf: Puffed out part of a dress, particularly over the bustle.

Pout-de-soie: A rich corded silk; also spelled poult de soie.

Princesse: A gown shaped from shoulder to hem without breaking at the waist.

Quille: Tapered inset.

Redingote: Originally a man's riding coat, it is a long gown, fitted at the waist, and open down the front, worn over a skirt.

Reps: Fabric with closely spaced ribs running in the direction of the weft.

Revers: Lapel; also a turn back on a sleeve or skirt.

Richelieu guipure: Cutwork with buttonholed edges joined with bars.

Richelieu lace: Net with raised embroidery.

Ruche: A narrow band of fabric, net, or lace set in pleats or gathers.

Saxony lace: Lace made by machine-embroidering designs in a different fiber than that used for the ground, then treating the fabric so that the ground dissolves, leaving the lace.

Sicilienne: A poplin woven with silk warp and fine wool weft.

Spiderweb toile: Darned lace applied to an open-work wool fabric.

Surah ècossais: Surah with a plaid pattern.

Surah: A soft twilled silk or wool, similar to foulard but heavier.

Tablier: An apron effect, usually draped, on the front of a skirt.

Thibet: Heavyweight wool dress or coat fabric.

Toque: A close-fitting brimless hat.

Torsade: Trimming or an ornament simulating a cord or rope.

Tussor: Fine corded cotton dress fabric.

Victoria: A kind of sicilienne with thick ribs.

Vigogne: A neutral-colored wool in a twill weave; alpaca.

Visite: Jacket closely fitting the body, with sleeves tight-fitting to the elbow, widening below.

No. 1

January 3, 1886

Left: Dress of sicilienne. Right: Visiting toilette.

No. 2

Ball coiffures.

January 10 , 1886

No. 3

Visiting toilettes.

January 17, 1886

No. 4

January 24, 1886

Left: Evening gown. Right: Short dress.

Fancy dress costumes.

No. 6

February 7, 1886

LEFT: Visiting toilette. RIGHT: Dinner toilette for young girl.

No. 7

February 14, 1886

Left: Dress of plush and faille. Right: Promenade toilette.

No. 8

February 21, 1886

LEFT: Dinner toilette. RIGHT: Promenade dress.

No. 11

March 14, 1886

LEFT: Dress of faille and cobweb toile. RIGHT: Dress of aloe cloth.

No. 12

March 21, 1886

Left: Toilette for a young woman. Right: Dress of tussor foulard.

No. 13

March 28, 1886

Left: Robe Colbert. Right: Costume of glacé silk and Flemish lace.

No. 14

April 4, 1886

Left: Visiting toilette. Right: Toilette for the races.

Leroy, imp. Paris.

No. 15

April 11, 1886

Summer hats.

No. 16

April 18, 1886

Town toilettes.

Leroy. imp. Paris.

Dinner toilettes.

No. 18

May 2, 1886

LEFT: Spring toilette. RIGHT: Toilette for the races.

LEFT: Promenade toilette. RIGHT: Toilette for the races.

Leroy, imp. Paris

No. 21   May 23, 1886

LEFT: Toilette for visiting or the races. RIGHT: Dress of etamine.

No. 22

May 30, 1886

Children's toilettes.

No. 23

Casino toilettes.

June 6, 1886

No. 24

June 13, 1886

LEFT: Costume of batiste-zephyr. RIGHT: Dress of sheer lawn and faille.

No. 25

June 20, 1886

LEFT: Promenade dress. RIGHT: Toilette for the races.

No. 26

June 27, 1886

LEFT: Dress of etamine. RIGHT: Dress of surah.

LEFT: Toilette of leze orientale. RIGHT: Toilette of cotton crepon and matching lace.

No. 28

July 11, 1886

LEFT: Toilette for the races. RIGHT: Seaside toilette.

LEFT: Costume of etamine and velvet. RIGHT: Costume of surah.

LEFT: Toilette for the casino and summer visits. RIGHT: Seaside toilette.

No. 31

August 1, 1886

LEFT: Seaside toilette. RIGHT: Toilette of surah and faille française.

LEFT: Casino toilette. RIGHT: Dress of canvas cloth.

LEFT: Short costume of bengaline and faille française. RIGHT: Toilette of faille française and net.

No. 34

August 22, 1886

LEFT: Costume of pongee. RIGHT: Costume of crepon and velvet.

No. 35

August 29, 1886

LEFT: Chateau toilette of grenadine. RIGHT: Promenade toilette of silk toile.

No. 36

September 5, 1886

LEFT: Costume of bengaline and velvet. RIGHT: Louis XIII costume for promenades and visiting.

No. 37

September 12, 1886

LEFT: Costume of figured surah. RIGHT: Costume of surah ecossais and cashmere.

No. 38

September 19, 1886

Hunting costumes.

No. 39

September 26, 1886

LEFT: Visiting dress. RIGHT: Traveling toilette.

No. 40

October 3, 1886

LEFT: Dress of double-faced faille française. RIGHT: Costume of etamine and velvet.

Winter hats.

No. 42

LEFT: Toilette for visiting and little dinners. RIGHT: Costume of star cloth.

No. 43

October 24, 1886

Left: Toilette for visiting and promenades. Right: Promenade toilette.

No. 44

October 31, 1886

Left: At-home toilette. Right: Costume of sicilienne.

No. 45

LEFT: Costume of pout-de-soie and thibet. RIGHT: Visiting toilette.

No. 46

November 14, 1886

Children's costumes.

No. 47

November 21, 1886

LEFT: Costume of velvet and sicilienne. RIGHT: Costume of velvet and bengaline.

LEFT: Promenade and visiting toilette. RIGHT: Visiting toilette.

No. 49

December 5, 1886

LEFT: Bridal toilette. RIGHT: Dress of faille.

No. 50

December 12, 1886

Ball gowns.

No. 51

December 19, 1886

Left: Costume of plush. Right: Costume of velvet.

No. 52

December 26, 1886

LEFT: Visiting toilette. RIGHT: Dress of faille française.